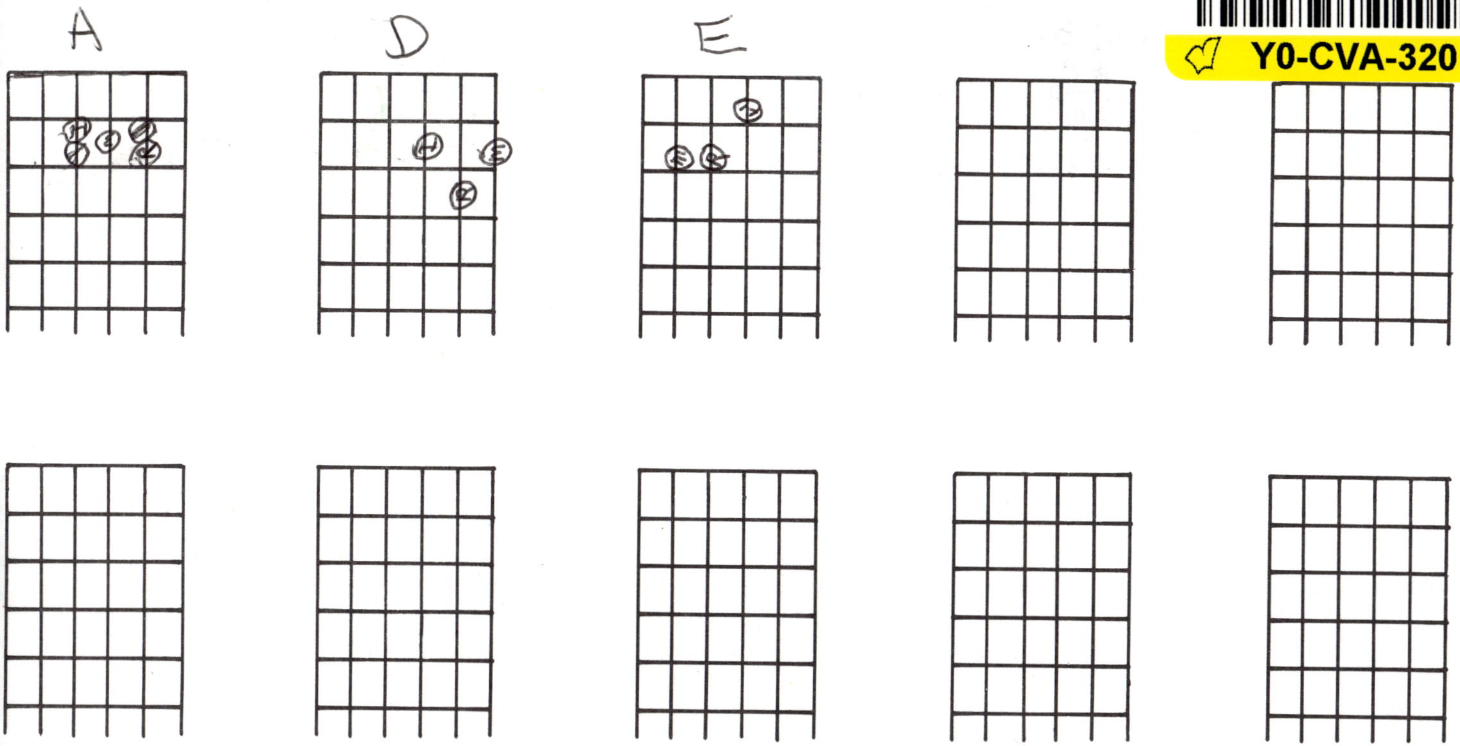

1 case of oil

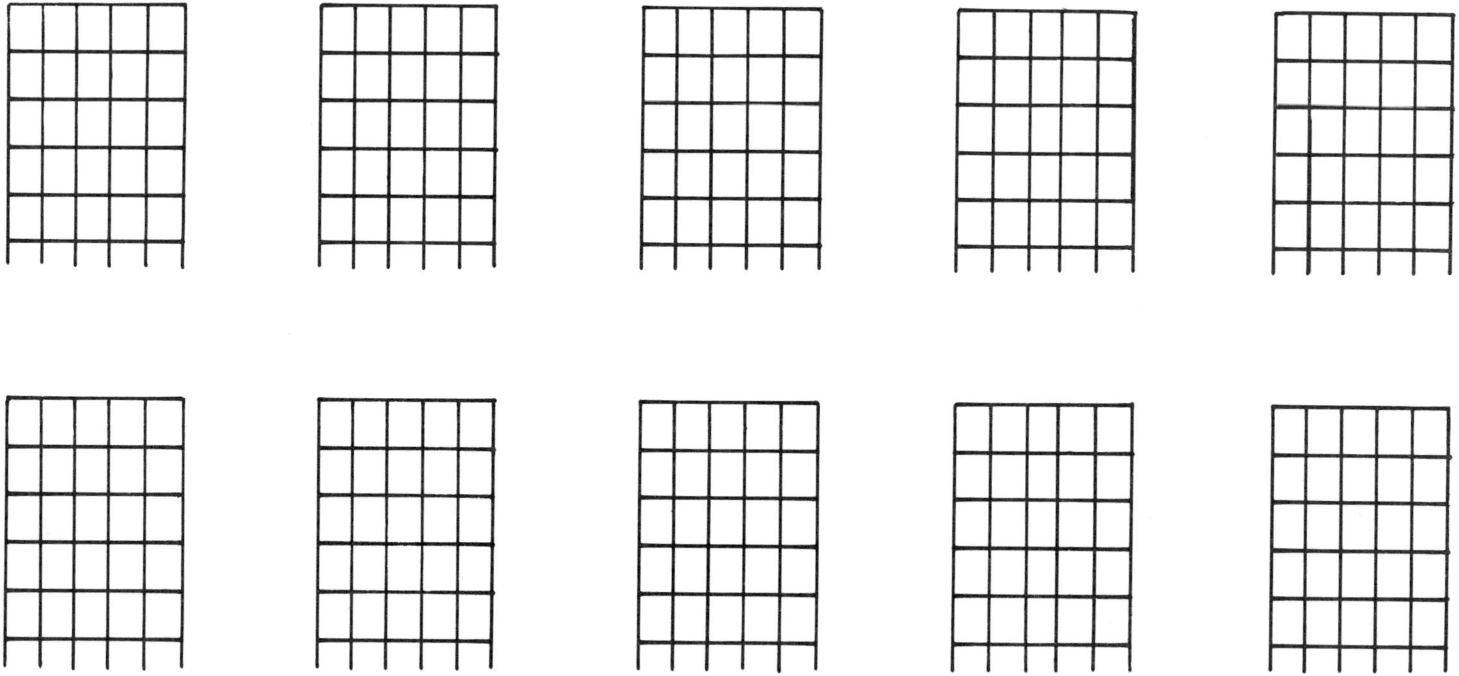

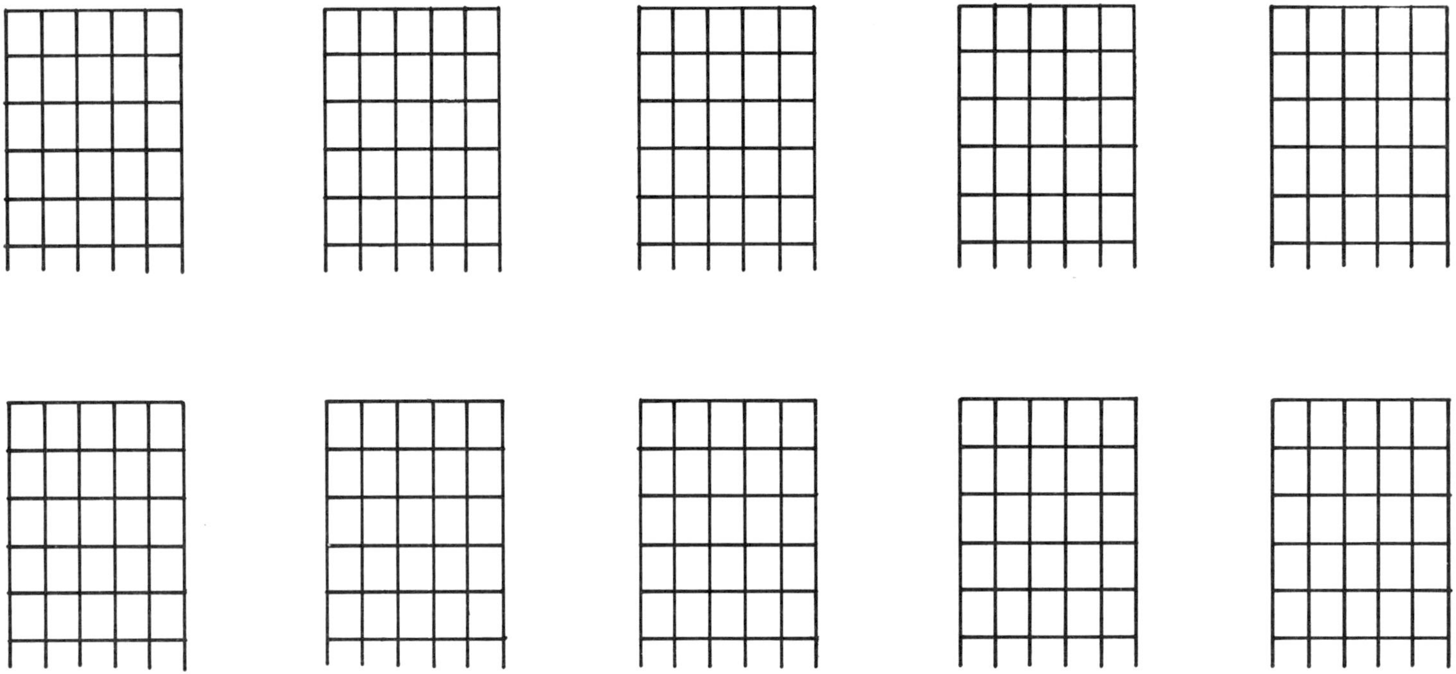

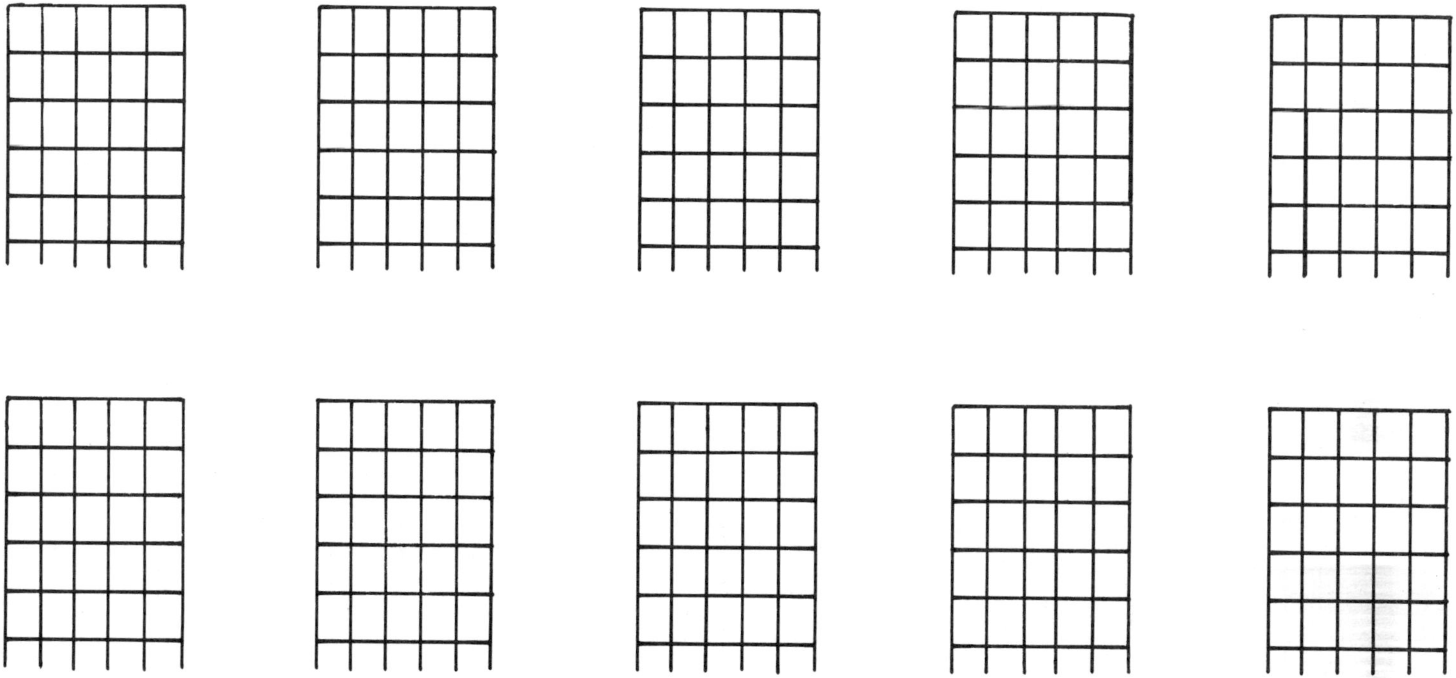

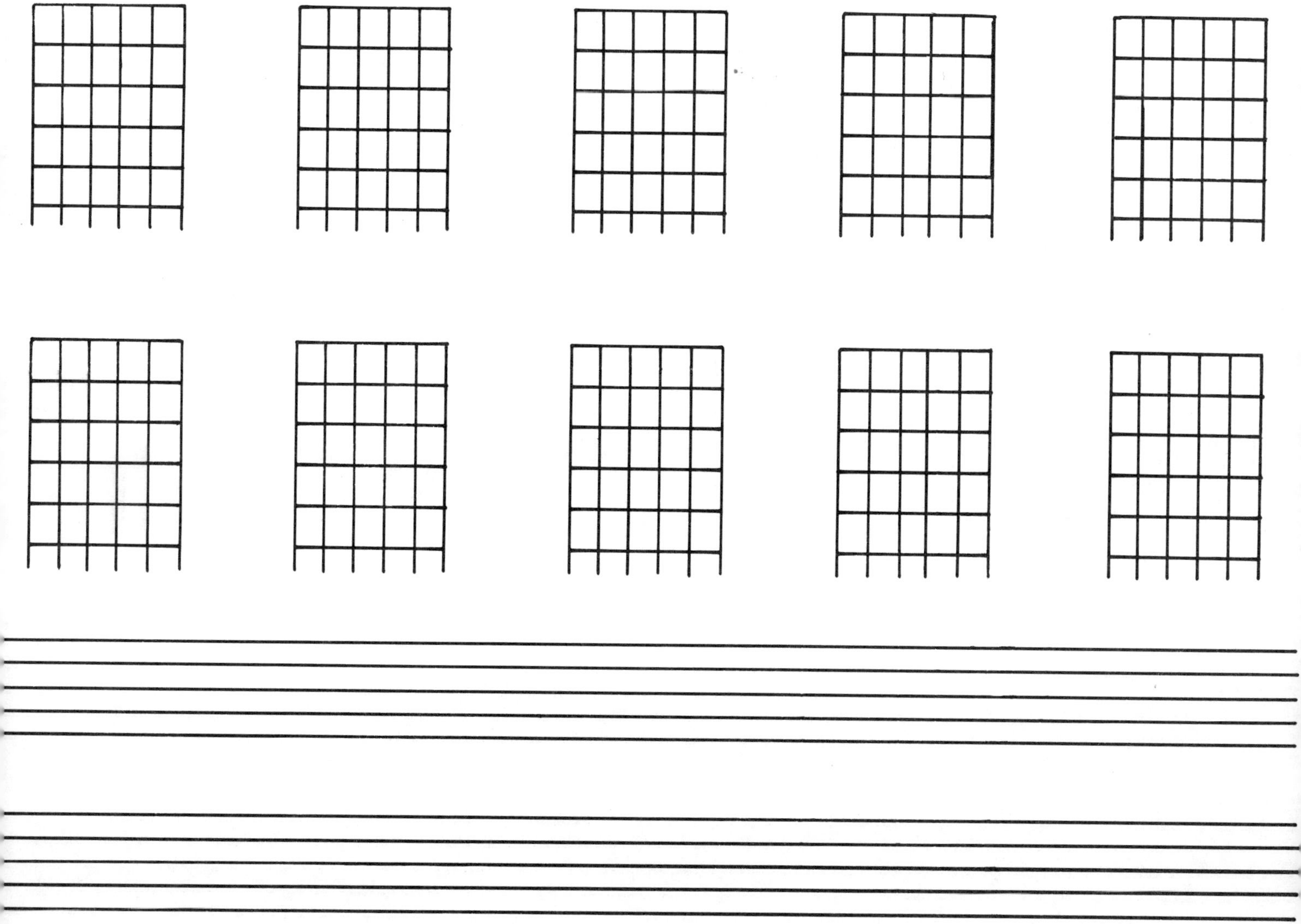

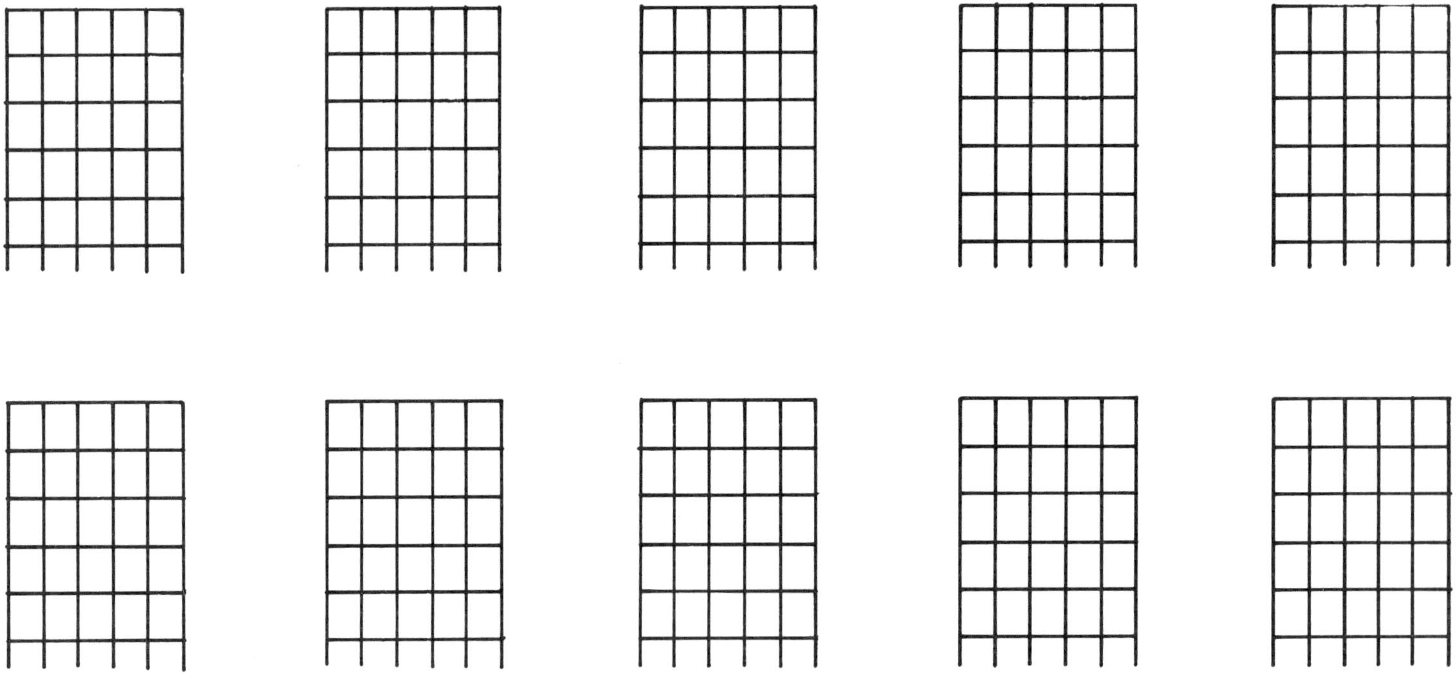

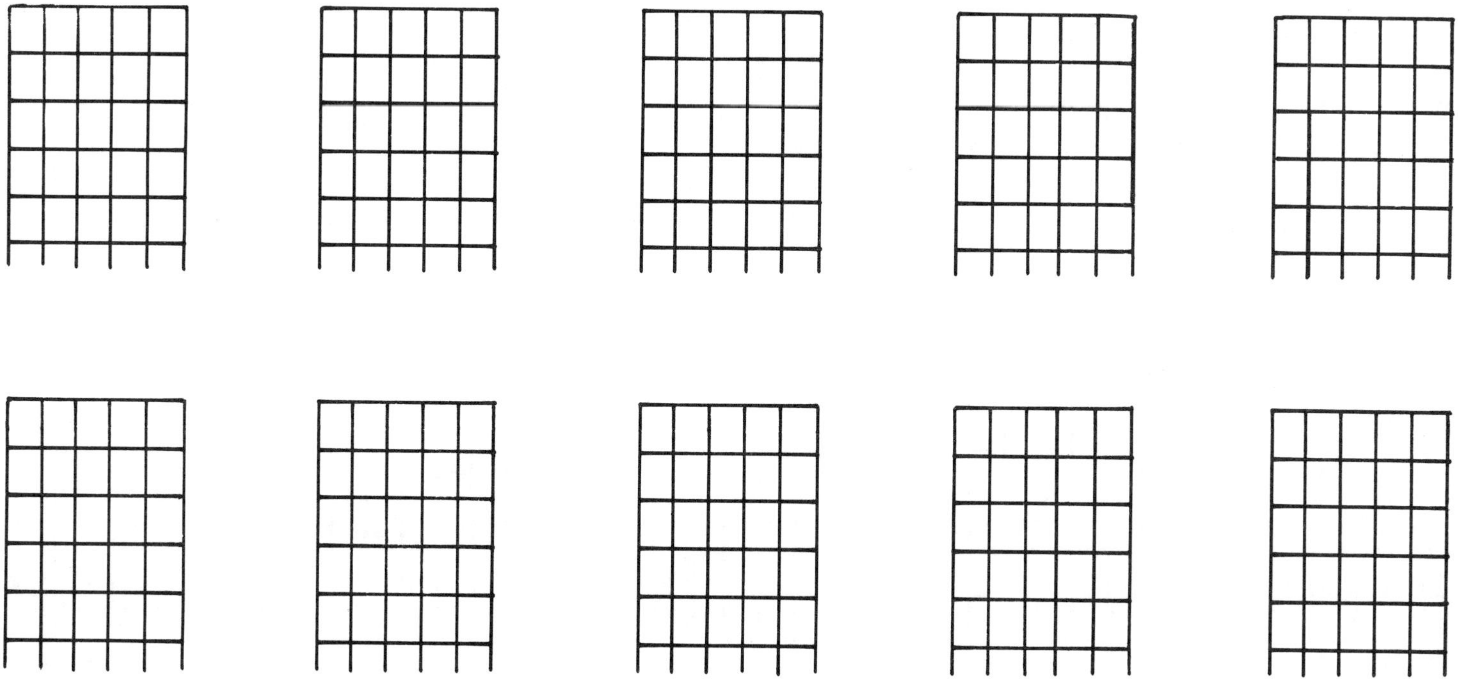

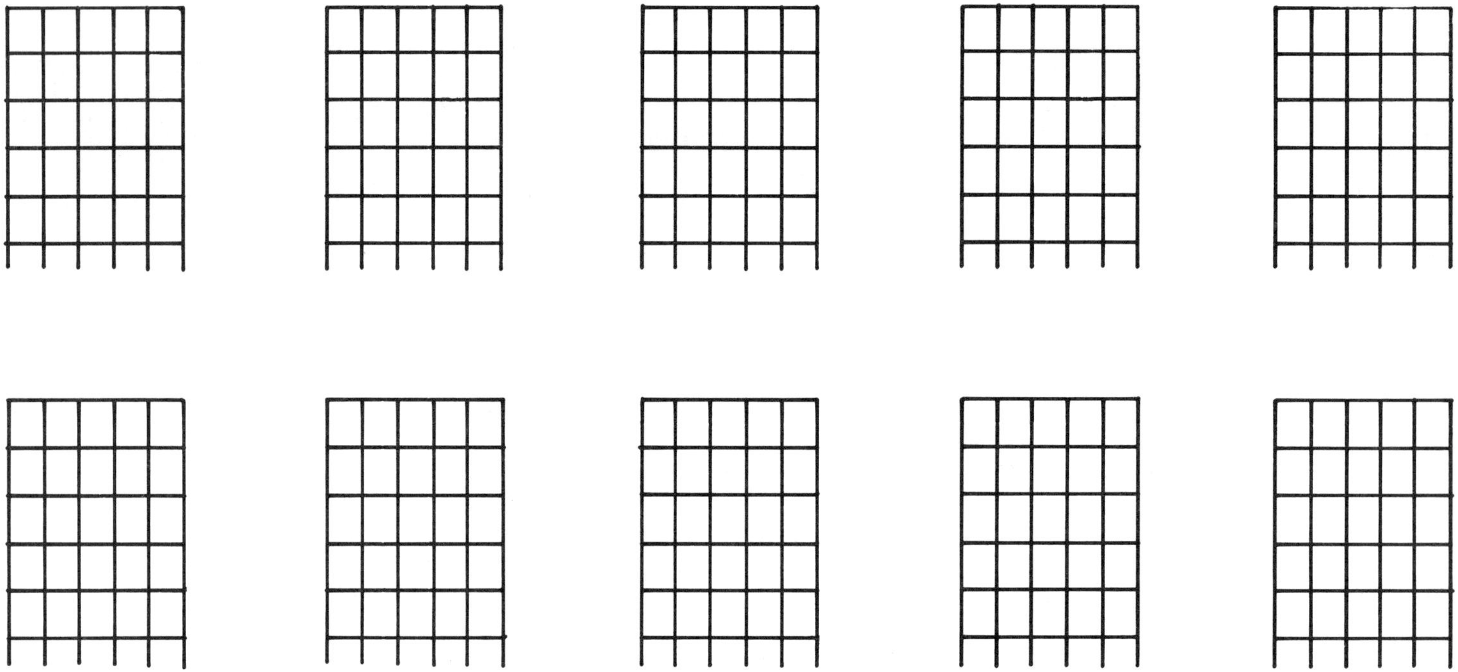

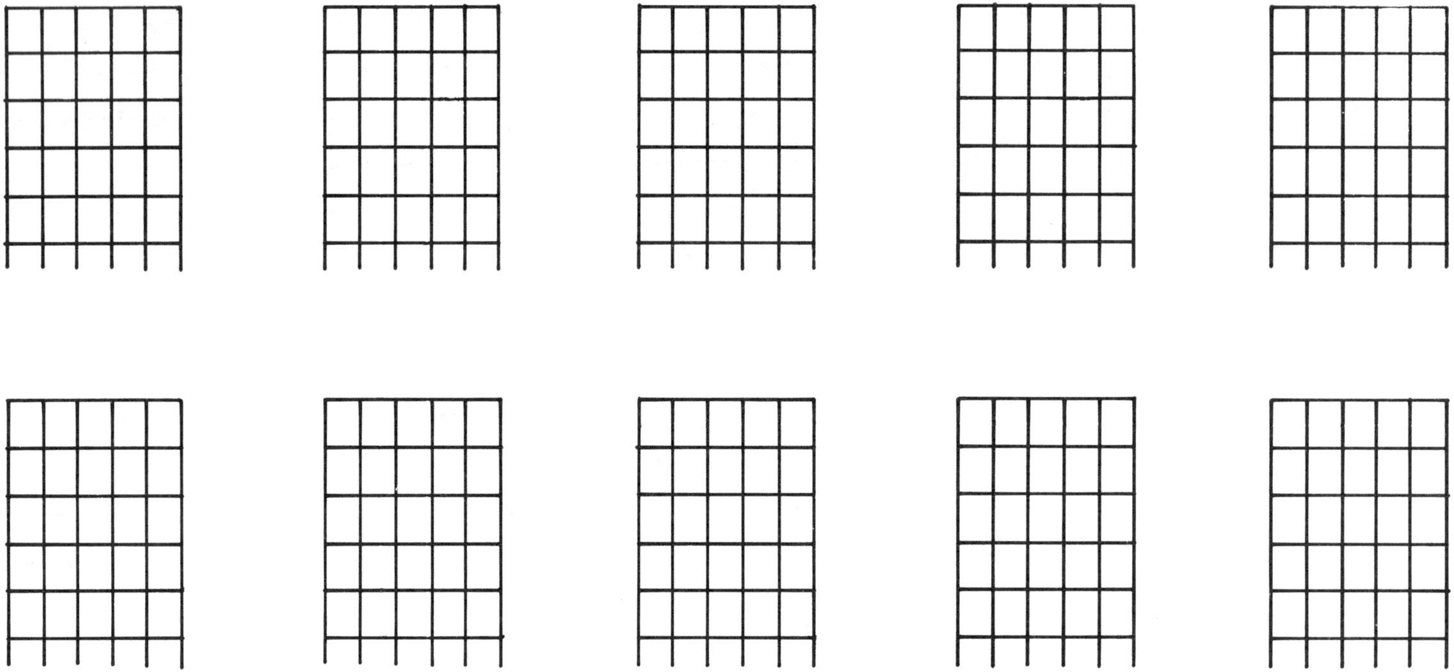

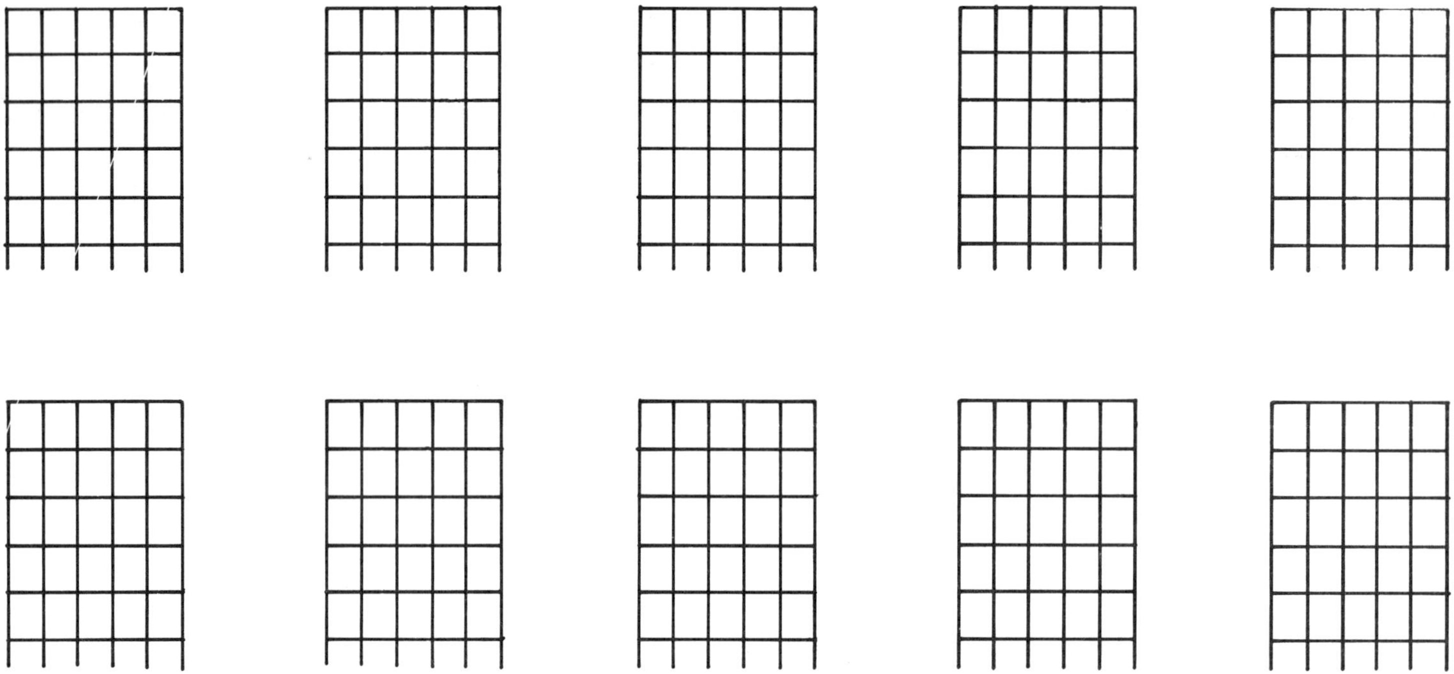

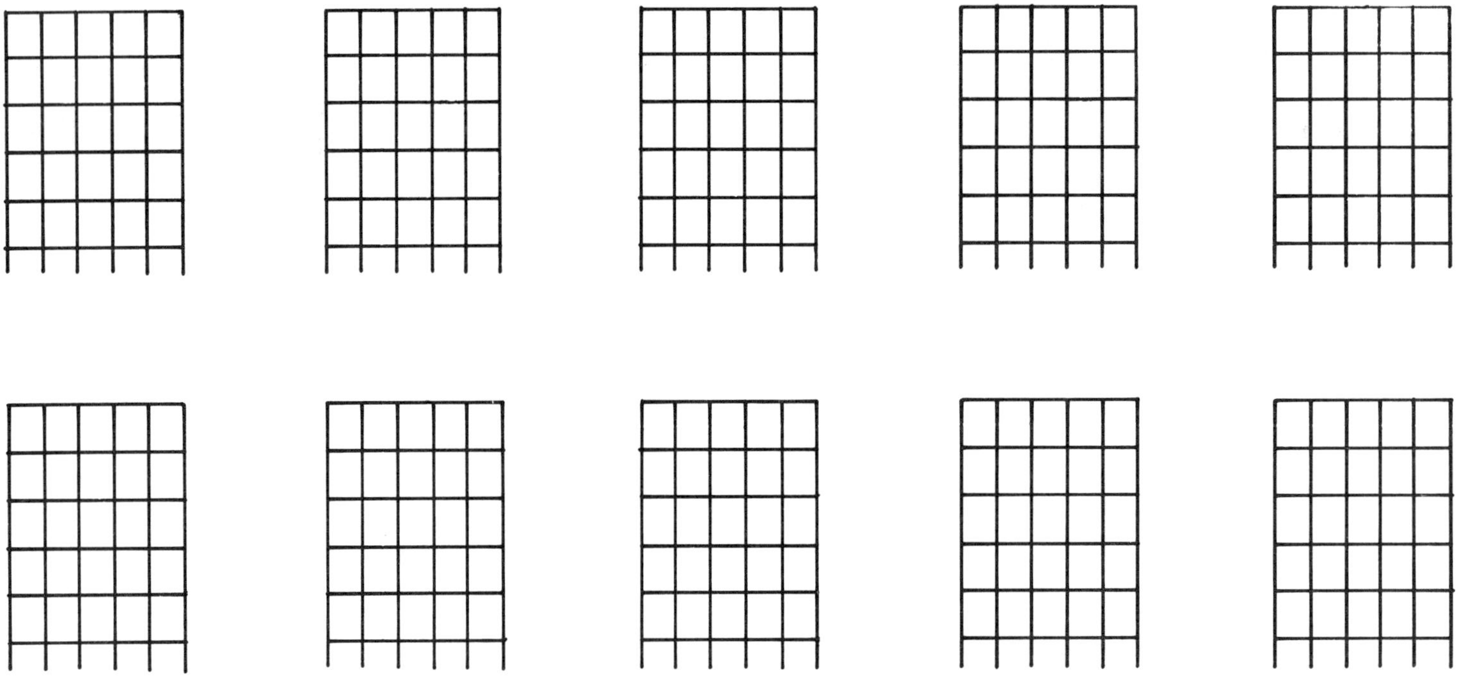

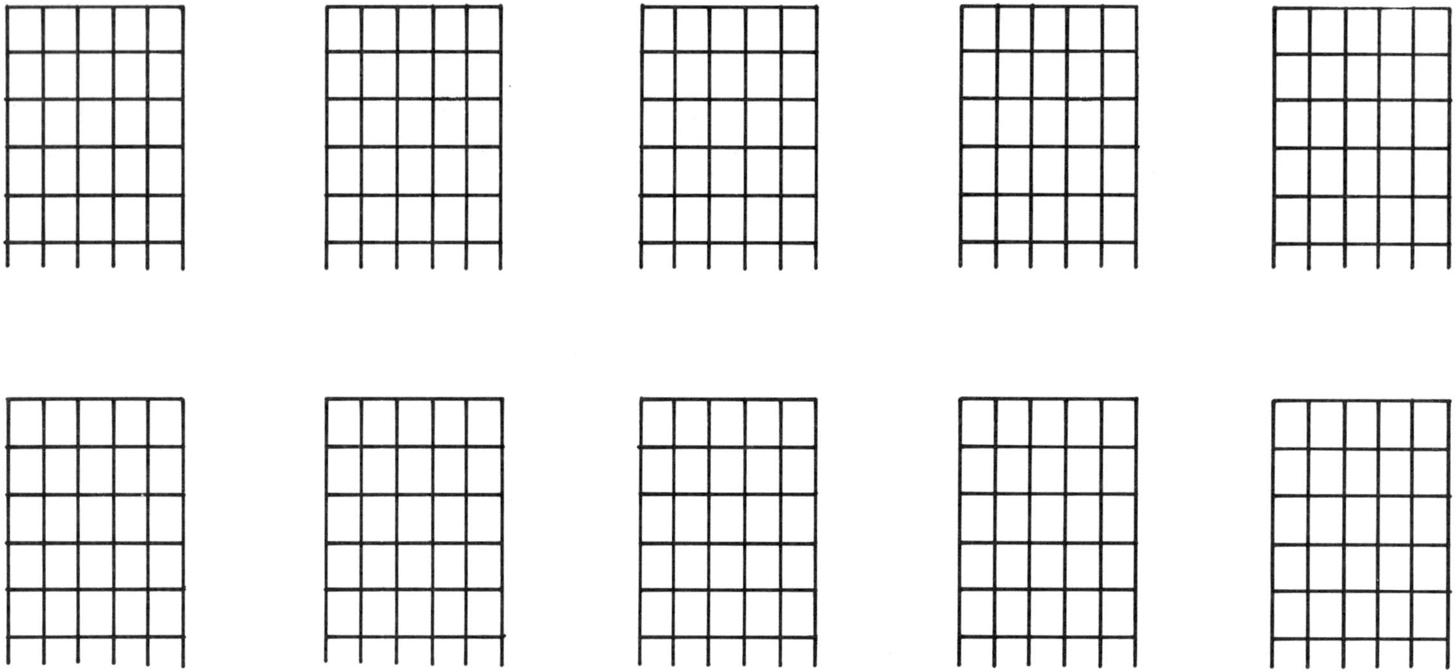

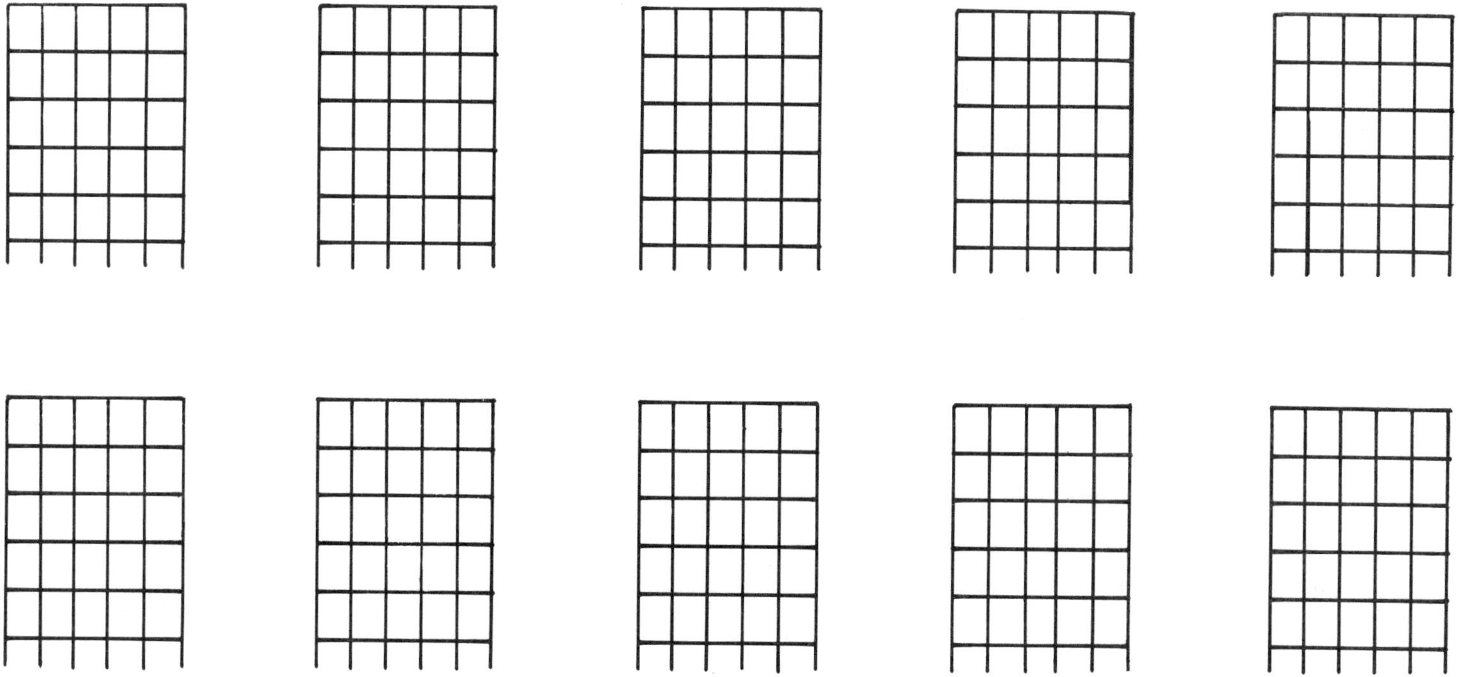